PRIVACY ISSUES

Privacy Issues

Poems by
Austin Alexis

LOTUS PRESS

Detroit

First Edition

International Standard Book Number 978-0-9797509-8-4

Printed in the United States of America

LOTUS PRESS, INC.
"Flower of a New Nile"
Post Office Box 21607
Detroit, Michigan 48221

www.lotuspress.org

Acknowledgments

Thanks are due to the editors of the following publications in which poems in this volume first appeared, sometimes in slightly different versions:

Journals:
"Accused" in *FutureCycle Poetry*
"Advice Before Surgery" in *Carcinogenic.com*
"After the Diagnosis" in *Lips*
"Agoraphobia" in *Acoustic Levitation*
"Bette Davis in the Box" in *Home Planet News*
"Dance Fragments" and "September the Eleventh" in *First
          Literary Review—East*
"Demons" in *Danse Macabre*
"Drag Queen" in *The Rogue Gallery/RogueScholars.com*
"Duck at the Gulf Oil Spill" in *Poems for Living Water*
"Globe" in *Poetz.com*
"H.I.V." in *The Cherry Blossom Review*
"The Janitor" and "The Tailor" in *Mobius: The Poetry Magazine*
"Merce Cunningham Event" in *Shot Glass Journal*
"Privacy Issues" in *Big City Lit*
"Power" in *Barrow Street*
"The Procedure" in *Paterson Literary Review*
"Protection" in *Phoenix*
"Relic" in *Brooklyn Arts Council 9-11 Archive*
"The Rosebush" in *The Journal*
"Survivor" in *The Other Magazine*
"Ten Hours After" in *Candelabrum Poetry Magazine (UK)*
"Twin Towers" in *The Pedestal Magazine*
"Watching a Psychopath" in *Red River Review*

Anthologies:
"Witness" in *And We the Creatures* (Dream Horse Press, C. J.
          Sage, editor)
"Edge of the Sea" in *The Brownstone Poets Anthology*
          (Brownstone Series Publication, Patricia Carragon,
          editor)

"Trans Beach Party" in *Come Hear!* (The Poet's Salon: Rainbow
    Book Fair Publication, Regie Cabico and Nathaniel A.
    Siegel, editors)
"Solar Panels" in *Dinner with the Muse* (Ra Rays Press, Evie
    Ivy, editor)
"Eyes" in *Off the Cuffs: Poems by and About the Police* (Soft
    Skull Press, Jackie Sheeler, editor)
"Roommates" in *Pears, Prose & Poetry* (Eggplant
    Press, Caitlin Foster and Roxanne Hoffman, editors)

Four of these poems were first published, in different versions, in
the chaplet, *Lovers and Drag Queens* (Poets Wear Prada Press,
Hoboken, New Jersey). Two of these poems first appeared, in
slightly different versions, in the chapbook, *For Lincoln & Other
Poems* (Poets Wear Prada Press, Hoboken, New Jersey).

"The Janitor" received the Editor-in-Chief's Award from
    Mobius: The Poetry Magazine.
"The Fall" was nominated for a Pushcart Prize by Poets Wear
    Prada Press.

Thanks to the Vermont Studio Center for an Artist Grant and a
Work-study Fellowship, including space and quiet, and to the
Helene Wurlitzer Foundation of New Mexico for a residency and
for general support.

Contents

II

III

Perfect purity is possible
if you turn your life
into a line of poetry
written with a splash of blood.

—Yukio Mishima

I

Pistol

It accomplishes
what an electric chair does,
but swifter.

It's more powerful
than an arrow,
more efficient than
a gas chamber.

Different from a lethal injection
of a clear poisonous liquid,
it is hard and dark—
a devilish finger.

It seduces a hand
with metal warm
and heavy as dirt at a gravesite.
Black as a dung-beetle's back
or a raven's feathers,
it is mysterious
even in unobstructed sunlight.

Once it is used
it leaves residue
on the user
like a score of sins
no savior can erase.

The Gunman
*(A gunman in Connecticut went on a shooting rampage before
being shot to death by law enforcement officials)*

Swollen with rage
he morphs into a huge ball
bouncing off concrete, asphalt, wood, flesh,
leaving bowling ball bodies knocked out,
sprawled at his feet.
What he perceives as lies,
what he sees as racism,
what he knows as betrayal
fills him with an excitable gas
to the ballooning point
where stillness is impossible;
motion is all.

He propels himself
or is shot forward by a force
old as the Atlantic and the Hudson combined:
the ancient sin of grinning injustice
which rarely fails to ignite insanity.
And the notion of shrugging off insults?
Don't be insulting.

He lunges into a future
safe from harassment
and beyond the range of all triggers.
Call him Son of Satan
but know in death

he has become
one with the cosmos,
its blank, unnamable face.

Techno

All hooked up to electronic gadgets,
wire in an earlobe,
wire around a hip,
damn wire cascading past a shoulder
toward a device near the crotch.

Not nicotine-free or sugar-free
but force-labor-chained to the latest
buzz, current, click and digit,
the with-it gimmicks of today.

Electro-magnetic fields don't surround you
like a saint's nimbus
but encase you like a sarcophagus—
a twenty-first century tomb.

Witness

Scientists, who consider themselves wise,
conspire in a lab.
The sanitized whiteness of their lab coats
does not blind me
to the stain of their deed:
the enticement of minute mice
unto death, to verify newfangled theories.

I spy the Corinthian jumble,
sad sculptural lump
of pale rodent tails
commingled, as in the closeness of love—
or an accelerated eagerness
to aid each other
before their clinical holocaust.

Central Park

Gargling beige leaves that rattle
on walkways, across boulders,
and hiss in the depths of maples.

Once a settlement for free blacks.
Once a fragrant but failed farm.
Once a high green site
where dignitaries dined.

Feminine lagoons hosting ducks
alluring as swans.
Masculine streams
penetrating their grooves.

Playland for orchestras and lovers.
Cool green rugs for those of modest means
to concert and picnic and frolic.
A rich man's siesta-land.

Home of hiding raccoons
and the flamboyant homeless
and energetic mosquitoes drilling through denim.
Resting place for sun rays
tired of steel and chrome.

Incarceration

Two female prisoners,
their wrists crisscrossed and handcuffed
and rested on their asses,
their elbows jutting out—ineffectual wings—
their gender nearly erased
in the efficiency of justice.

Some-kind-or-other officer
leads them from a building
to a squad car.
His face registers neutral.
The prisoner on the right
smirks in witty anger.
The one on the left
wears the hungry, aggrieved look of a hamster
caged and mazed in a lab.
During this and any other afternoon
the aura of criminality is calm
then cheerful, then desperate
all at once.

Where they are going
is where the world stands still,
a place where their crimes
exert a gravity their legs will try to outwit,
strive to defy,
yet never will.
Wind does not go there. No hint of motion.
Their location, a gray boulder,

a dry outcrop,
will exist without orbits or rotation—
a planet deprived of a sun.

Last Days

There, at the planet's core,
churning in red anger
in a world beyond speech,
a ton of guilt
weighs down Mother Earth.
She has gone through many stages
to reach this defeat.
It's been so hard
to try to be a good parent;
she has achieved the grade of "F."
Her heart beats—haunted.
Failure boils in her molecules,
her shamed-faced atoms.
Pollution reigns; rains of acid fall.

Now, she thinks of nothing
except to disintegrate,
create a fire fierce enough
to burn stone,
to extinguish her womb of lava,
to erase the longing for immortality
and embrace the blankness
that waits
at the end of time.

Globe

Time only seems infinite;
it is as finite as the earth
and the earth has only one life
just like a person,
just like a cell.

The planet has taken this time
to check itself into a critical ward.
But critical does not mean fatal.
Each of us is a doctor.
Each of us, a nurse.

Solar Panels

Strike them. They're dense.
Maybe heavy. Definitely smooth.
They draw energy
odorless as a god
and clutter-free,
grime-free,
free of gray soot
and smutty smog
and off-brown dirt.
They emit no sound
as they convert rays
during a holy task.
Diligent as nuns,
wanting nothing back,
these surfaces receive,
then give.
If they could speak,
hushed as chanted Latin
would be their tenor.
If they could disobey,
they wouldn't.
What furnace or engine
ever worked
with so little grumbling?

Accused

You sit in prison for a crime
you didn't commit:
wrong multiplied to the tenth degree,
to the twentieth power.
First, you glow with indignation;
you drag it; it drags you.
You feel top-heavy with rage
so you topple over
into a region of disbelief
where nothing computes as real—
a fantasy land.
Your eyebrows freeze into question marks.
Then you steer your mind
toward a lucid zone,
commanding reason and facts
to drive you out of madness.

Later you reach for a rosary
as a person who's fallen overboard
flails for a life preserver
or as a drowning child
tries to grab a wave,
striving to make it stay still,
hoping to make it turn solid.

Finally you land on anger,
anger again.
You come ashore on its hot sand strip.
It's ablaze, and you are at home.

You're fired up with musings,
your sizzling past scorching the present.

The future stays bathed in harsh rays,
blinding you.
(Justice seems sightless in its own stupidity.)
Even shading your eyes
you can't penetrate beyond the glare
to stare into tomorrow.
And you can't get anyone else
to look in that direction, either.

Watching a Psychopath

You concentrate
on the meek-brown color of his hair
as he stands humbly
in the eyes of the courtroom,
a mere thirteen feet away from
the strangle of your fingers.

You concentrate
on what you imagine is
the feather weight
of his hair on his forehead
to keep from musing on
the heft of those blows
he delivered to your brother,
the cracked skull he caused. The death.

You concentrate
on how ordinary he looks
bagged in orange prison garb
and sweet-sour sweat—
the rancid look of him, smug,
as if he's eaten and disgusted
the monster that was his soul
and all that remains is
his sated body greedily breathing
the air it doesn't deserve.

Broadcast

The latest tragedy
in high definition
just as you want it.
The recent massacre
sunny-side up.
With conditioner-enhanced hair,
scrumptious-looking fingernails
and Garbo-perfect makeup,
I impart the news
(in all its diverting gruesomeness).
Innocent-eyed, I present the buzz of it
belting it out in my upbeat voice.
My clothes are trendy,
my manner so friendly.

You have the need to know,
to be brought near
to far-away catastrophes.
Monitor me: I'm as close to disasters
as I am to lollipops of metal
I speak into with my wagging tongue.
I bring the news and amuse
in my A-plus
Public Speaking 101 Course tone.
You pant, hungry for my servings.
You expect information
wrapped in festive gift paper,
the dire stuff neatly sealed

like slightly stale preserves in a jar,
neutral as a defused bomb,
sugared so it'll do no harm.

Privacy Issues

Corporations want to know
what I do
and when I do it,
crave stacks of information:
my zip code, for instance,
and the number of light bulbs I own,
and the precise weight
of the dust under my bed, et cetera.

The first commandment of the market place says,
"Thou shall hand over thine underwear
for inspection, on cue."
But I finished cooperating with companies
like yesterday.
I am done giving away my resources.
I'm sick of cameras down my throat,
seeing my innards
but blind to their workings.

Oh, Corporate Grandpoppies,
stop going for my veins;
get out of my apartment.
Hands out of my savings account!
Leave my checkbook unmarked
and my sanity intact.
Go to the assassinating cold of Pluto.
Go study someone or something else:

the environment, for instance,
and stop yourself from
screwing it up.

Transit

Not that he held anything against
obese people.
But the narrow subway seat,
situated next to the heavy lady,
offered little room.

He took steps toward
that unoccupied stretch,
that slab of horizontal plastic,
then pivoted,
opted for the available space
opposite the fat woman.
Her eyes took in this plot twist.

The commute lasted and lasted.
The lady wore her expression
like unchanging stone.
He will never forget
the evasive stares
that traveled between them.

Tunnels

Deep in subway tunnels
rats roam in freedom,
a light coating of grime
protecting their itsy-bitsy feet.

Deep in subway tunnels
paintings sprawl, luminous with red,
translucent with orange
not vulnerable to dust
but transcending it.

Deep in subway tunnels
a worker clears debris from tracks,
fears oncoming trains,
their muscle-steel hit
potentially hurtling him to death.
As they approach he hears their screech,
the hunger in it
shoving him to fear
the way the first hunters and gatherers
knew by instinct to shake with fright,
flee big-pawed animals.
They learned to hide from predators
in caves
where they sought liberty from tyranny.

As their bodies tried to relax
they spread shapes on walls—

an oval, a crescent,
red, orange—
to soften the dark.

Survivor

(for victims of Haiti's earthquake)

Pulled out, alive,
from beneath the rubble
of mud, slumbering lumber,
oppressive concrete clumps,
you are a poem
a poet has fashioned
with a hallelujah ending,
a song that simmers
then explodes with mirth,
a canvas splashed
with dashes from every rain-color-bow
that ever arched
over the Amazon, the Mississippi,
the perfumed Nile.

Shiny fellow,
new as the dawn,
novel as a ghost,
your footsteps don't thud
but ring out—
a surprise—a steeple gone wild.

Ten Hours After
(for September the 11th))

Smoke floats, travels northeast,
charcoals the sunset air.

Skyscrapers have given in
to evil, the tragattacks, crude terror.

Gothic the landscape, the sprawled limbs, heaps—
reign of debris where order has fled

leaving only blunt juttings
of beams, unmoored from structures,

groping through holocaust hours, outstretched,
dramatizing their karma, their defeat
like lost trails of smoke . . . .

Relic

in memory of 9-11-01

Her body was incinerated
when one of the planes
crashed into the floor
above the floor
where she worked every weekday,
devoted to emails, memos, files.

Only her open-toed shoe remains.
Even the strap at the back
came through intact.
Authorities solemnly gave
the stylish sandal
to her numb husband.
He has placed it
where she usually housed favorite items:
on the left, gracing her closet floor.

Miraculous, even freaky,
it endures the shame of having survived
by merely continuing to exist
after the holocaust.
It proves to be
less fragile than a human
and strong enough
to carry a person's spirit.

Twin Towers

I remember
your cool sleek side,
the efficiency
of your invincible
verticality,
that thrust—
victorious—
into the sky.

The roar
of your death
as you crashed
echoed
the bustle
of your life:
vital collages of people
glass, chrome,
cable light.

Heavy metal,
don't appear again
in my mind's eye,
alive yet
creating two
tombstones
too difficult
to erase—
the sketches
of steel ghosts.

September the Eleventh

1.
Waiting to be saved
on the ninety-fifth floor . . . .
waiting for nearby clouds
to turn into parachutes . . . .

2.
Even my cat
statued in a corner
sensed the globe's face
        had dropped;
the world would never again
manage its old smile.

3.
Since 9-11 I cannot
spot a plane anywhere—
in a sky, on a runway—
without noticing
its huge shadow.

Power

One drop on your skin
and you're dead within minutes
(two or three)—
like a fall
into a pit of quicksand.
Biological. Weapons.
Pretty words. Words
that should be kept apart.
Like a splash of lava
one minuscule drop
corrodes and scalds.
Then one knows misery
similar to a whale's
knowledge of the icy allegro
stab of a harpoon
or a fish's sense of
arrogant power:
air without water.

Duck at the Gulf Oil Spill

I should not feel vulnerable.
Something or someone with my poise,
my fine-tuned confidence,
should cruise the waterway
and own it.
Instead, I fret and pose,
a static pieta,
my son and I
stricken with a substance
inescapable as sundown.

Doomed to never fly again
the two of us wobble,
attempting to lurch across
sand, tattered sand,
an expanse of sand deranged
into a diseased image of itself.
Surveying it, we witness
an echo of ourselves:
once majestic, now pathetic.

Weak as shredded seaweed
we await hands to squeeze us,
to drain oil off our slick sides,
our gooey tummies,

our stuck beaks,
our immobile wings.

We drop pride
as we once shed feathers.

The Janitor

Every weekday at 9:03 a.m.
we hear his music,
the clank this sad man's pan makes
hitting against the hall's fake marble;
the swish of his broom
just beyond our kitchen door;
his shoes' hard-angry thud
on steps, on littered landings.
We imagine his melancholy face
inclined over his tasks,
his mustache handles drooping
like two huge dirty tears.

When he has finished for the day
he must picture being done, emancipated
for the rest of his life.
Free, free at last
to buy a thousand Snickers Bars,
watch the games forever,
pinch his wife for the next twelve hours.
Trumpet-shouts of hurray
resound in his mind,
prod his lips
out of their numb exhaustion.
Like a comic strip character
balloons of festive dialogue
halo his head.
Unlike a comic strip
the pronouncements don't stay

imprisoned in a page's pores
but shirk off their confinement.
They release themselves into the world.
Audible, maybe even happy swear words,
they seem to him syllables of scripture
as they choir the air
every weekday at 5:03 p.m.

The Tailor

Each morning you rise at 6:00 a.m.
to go where you were
the evening before.
Every day starting at 7:00 a.m.
you help buttons
find their destinies
on sleeves, on strips.
Zigzagging the thread of your life
you stitch a wallet for yourself.

Cloth and pants mountain your counters.
You are used to climbing
the tasks of mending, adjusting.
You are to fabric
what glass is to a window frame.
Legs and arms test your skills
and your patience,
your rulers and your thumbs.

At 7:10 p.m. you close shop
inevitably, like a late-day sun
inching to its customary bed
or a tide tied to
the rhythm it must not break.
The sky models its El Greco dusk
through your shop window
as you count your bills
with the reliability of a clock
measuring its daily dose of minutes.

II

About Dickinson

You exist as an elm, growing
in a garden you've cultivated.
You, tangle of thick branches,
hurt no one.
No one hurls
lightning bolts toward you.

Free from outer conflict
you wrestle with
inner goddesses of turmoil.
But you, too, own the weapons,
the strategies of a deity.
War zones of the interior
you are acquainted with,
as fireflies know the night
and use their glow like pistols,
piercing the threatening dark.

Combat becomes your living theater.
Images convert into your rifles.
Syllables, phrases:
your techniques of battle.
You alone position cannons.
Alone, you blast forth,
conquering angst
with an explosion of words.

Bette Davis in the Box

Slinking across the TV screen
in black and white
lurid as El Greco colors,
you titillated as you mesmerized.
I scrutinized: my firefly
captured in a jar and lighting it up;
my specimen: alive
in the microscope slide,
the captioned glass of late night television.

"Nobody swings their butt
better than Bette Davis,"
another celebrity said.
I liked the taste of that truth.
Hypnotized by your bold hesitant stride,
those bouncing hips, that strut,
I stayed up till 2:30 a.m.
watching you outshine
the glare of a full moon.
Who else possessed
your drop-dead, slam-bang diction?
Who else wielded your ability to morph
from prostitute to governess to southern belle?
Oh murderess, oh heiress,
I didn't know what sleep was
when you appeared on Channel 13 or 9,
in makeup or nearly without,
throwing a diva tirade
or looking spiritual and kind.

High school days inched along
at a boring pace
compared to my nights
enthralled by sun rays
beaming from *Dark Victory.*
I didn't mean to ignore my parents.
However, defeated, they knew their place,
trudged off to their shadowed bed,
their tired voices muttering,
"That B.D. lady likes to show herself."
"So-o-o?" I asked or said, defensively,
pupils still gazing screenward toward you
the way eyes once stared upward
at mass hallucinations,
not wanting to differentiate
the real from the imagined.

The Beatles' American Debut

The theater ushers coach you
to understand
it's all right to scream
to show you like someone.
Eager for the program,
your back tingling,
your blood thumping in your throat,
ears radar-keen,
pupils stronger than ex-rays,
you discover
hair is a clean mop;
a head is a tongue
bouncing in a joyous bell
seized by harmony.

Rapture isn't Saint Theresa
leaning back, pierced and enthralled.
Rapture isn't
a philosopher, wide-eyed,
riveted by an insight.
Rapture is a stage
thrust forward with guitars, with drums,
the beat: a heart, a heart.
You'd die to keep that pulse thrumming
intertwined with melodies
echoing from a better world.
Those catchy lullabies
help you grow back to childhood.
You'd stay an infant for eons

to keep the songs from ending.
The notes massage you,
are hands you want to hold.

Merce Cunningham Event

Dance is ephemeral

each step says
as it disappears . . . .

These movements exist as
fey flights of hummingbirds,
dangling life of dragonflies
magnified, then erased . . . .

Simultaneous sequence.
Quick glitterings.
Shards of glass
enjoying their fragmentation
as an audience sifts through
this elaborate puzzle,
letting set pieces fall
wonderfully out of place.

Elegy for Balanchine

The secular religion of dance
sings a hymn
trimmed in purple.
Those melodic lines fill a plaza
otherwise austere,
even barren.
The plaza's fountain
forgets to heave its vigorous suds
or has lost the muscle.
Minutes, inching hours,
linger . . . try to step
from morning to afternoon.

Stark as an expanse of water
the stretch of day
gradually ebbs toward night
(as a river in stages dries,
becomes a bed of desolate soil).
Stark as an expanse of water
the day he died
fades to twilight
then dusk,
some light still visible
sheer as silk, chiffon,
rimming the horizon.

Dance Fragments

Strolling through the echoing lobby to a bank of elevators and taking one to the ninth floor where a class is about to begin. A dance class: a preview of heaven. No time to warm up. Just enough time to pull off street clothes (with dance garb already underneath) and plunge into movement. The swinging, the fall-and-recover motions make anybody who tries them glide into elation. Look at those grins. Middle-aged limbs feel a surge of invincibility. This qualifies as an in-body out-of-the-body experience. Sweat flies. Hearts pound, astonished by their own eager speed. How to sustain these sensations when not dancing is the question.

Motion

West Indian security guard,
ghosting a Lincoln Center corridor—
his uniform blending with the semi-dark—
tried rushing me out of the theatre
after a performance
pitched to the stratosphere.
Overweight and under-happy,
his frown drowning him,
he growled; he taunted.
He urged patrons forward
with fireman gestures,
my watchful highness,
authority in navy blue,
threatening yet somehow comic.

His sweep of the air
indicating the exits
couldn't whisk away visions
I'd just witnessed:
Helene Alexopoulos, fragrant,
pure liquid flesh,
splitting her body
as *The Nutcracker's* Arabian Dancer,
spreading her branches
in every delicious direction.
An apple tree, a fruit vine,
she climbed space and my memory,
etched lines only a sorceress could conjure.

My feet moved, but lingered.
Balletic witchery pirouetted
in my fugue-brain, rewinding,
reveling in contrary motion.
I was taking so long to leave
the gates were being drawn
(by a hunky grumbling usher)
locking me in like the bars of a jail
where prison feels better than descending
to the outside world.

Go-go Boy

You do nothing
except stand on a bar top
and subtly rock your hips.
You in your butterscotch skin.
You in your armor of muscles.
Ah, you in your near nudity
barely noticing who sits and watches you.

The audience you live for
comes to life when you appear
among the drinks and disco balls
and dollar bills—
all active objects
stirring and sprouting like erections.
In this theatre of beer,
with its dance club beams,
hands slipping money into jock straps,
into spandex shorts, into waistbands
resemble octopus limbs
in an ocean's undulating bliss.
See green-tinged busyness—
appendages amid sea weed strips of light—
all swelling for you,
you who do next to nothing.

Don't go, until the music
dims to 4:00 a.m. stillness,
till the bouncer comes in
to kick the patrons out.

Don't go with your alluring apathy
taking the pulled
longings hanging out of your gawkers
like red-hot entrails
ripped from dazed and wounded sailors.

H.I.V.

At some point one maybe two persons emerged:
the first ones to name it,
a disease that commenced to extinguish gay men
like an altar boy snuffing out candles.
Companions would no longer glow
with the light of camaraderie.
The weird condition would dampen,
wet their sparks, their lively flames.

Radio announcers must have uttered the name
scientists had given it:
initials, with an explanation,
like a T.V. station's moniker.
The announcer's poised syllables:
peacefully dangerous—a gas leak,
the soft-snaky workings of fumes.

A label with such power to shatter
cuts off music at parties,
dims chic lights low, so low, too low
for anything but panic, flight.
The lightning force of language
thundered as it taught its lesson:
devastation in a few consonants and vowels;
what lurks in the alphabet;
the brute muscles of sounds;
innocence betrayed
by a triplet of letters.

Trans Beach Party

Transsexuals on the sand
near a dazzle of waves,
in a surge of sun rays.
Proud of their breasts
and their stylized eyebrows.
Displaying painted toenails
no matter the lifeguards' frowns.

Over there and over there
the weirdly normal
wallow in conventionality.
Let bourgeois families
leave the shore in a rush—
a gusty wind of objection.
A hurricane huff.
Allow for insincere grins,
suspicious stares,
sunglasses turned into lenses of censor.

Gulls sailing in an air-stream
converge on nearby boulders.
Each one shrieks at invisible prey,
then sails toward humpy sand.
They glide, blind to wigs and shaved legs.
Clouds, content, doze in their blue.
A beach fly jerks through air,
dives for a bite of an arm
wanting flesh, regardless of gender.

Drag Queen

Sad in your happiness,
young-old in your looks,
you search for sources of energy
the way hyperactive nations
consume all consumables.
You long to get the energy you give.

You are fun, fabulous fun,
oh sweet honey, so much fun!
At 666 Deacon Place, a chic club,
you tickle the air.
At a party turned orgy
you become pure sitcom.
Who will entertain you
when you tire of titillating others?

Beat, yet
      intoxihigh,
            wig hair flying,
you strut 4:00 a.m. lanes
using luck to ward off predators,
wanting drugs to conjure contentment.
Hope fades as your makeup
disappears into flakes . . . smudges . . .
a mask refusing fine-tuning.

By dawn, your life's screen
resists all adjustments.
Color all gone,

the black-and-white picture weakens;
glaring static-snow thickens.

Eyes

When I saw the cop
and he saw me
in the dimly lit deli,
his brown-eyed gaze said
I was either a criminal or
a sex object.

Later, when he spotted me
and I glimpsed him
in the neon glow of my beloved
lower Second Avenue
I felt like Marilyn Monroe:
skirt blown up, exposed,

similar to white paper
revealing intimate words.
His granite stare—
a powerful badge—
knew no dimmer,
forgot moderation.

Like an officer
in the heat of giving a beating,
he crouched in a furnace,
a firestorm of emotion,
be it animosity
or forbidden love.

Altered

You become a new statue
re-sculptured, the way waves
reshape a shoreline.
You learn a new dialect,
syllables of swallowed vowels, hesitations.
Even without being touched
you have been molested.
Words all by themselves
brandish fingers, a grip, claws.

The texture of your life
corroded, you reach for the varnish
to paint over and hush
the language of shame.

Hitler's Adversaries

Plotting Hitler's death,
planning the festive event,
became their sacred experience.
What is an assassination
if not a murder
raised to the level of skyscraper loftiness,
to the stratosphere of moral imperative?

They felt so good about themselves.
They smiled and chuckled and smirked and chuckled
and grinned and chuckled some more.
The bomb they'd concocted
would go off at the time appointed—
the heroic contraption,
the god device
ready to change the future
for the inevitable better.
The first persons to perceive penicillin,
the primary shovelers hired to plow the Panama Canal:
those people mirrored Hitler's opponents,
all of them yodeling for joy,
waltzing across bright mountaintops.

Hitler dodging the boulder they rolled at him
didn't decimate the honey on their tongue,
the sweet, sweet hive they'd sampled
formulating their project,
believing it would work,
contemplating the solar system minus the devil.

Licking their saccharine fingertips
they beamed,
anticipating the re-creation of the world.

Goth: A Poem in Two Voices

Voice One:
>Are you The Devil?
>Your apartment glows,
>the red of hell.
>Your tongue, obsessive, flickers
>out of your mouth—a flame.
>Your body reminds me of a snake:
>that hairlessness, that suede feel.
>Worst of all, your genitals
>stay hidden. Or maybe don't exist.
>You can't be human.

Voice Two:
>You came with me to Hades
>but cleverly escaped.
>I salivate over the prospect of getting you
>back, stamped for murder.
>Your flesh will sweeten my mucus membrane
>as I grip your tendons with my AIDS-laced teeth.
>Who knows what quicksand lurks
>at the back of my throat.
>Baby, lock your door.

Roommates

People write poems about lovers
but rarely about roommates.
Take the roommate who reeks of revenge
because his roomer
won't be his lover.
Or the one who is a Blanche Dubois
wearing her cravings
like scarves that strangle,
sharing living quarters
with desire that's disaster.

Maybe all roommates are lovers, after all,
even if they avoid the most accidental touch
and seem peaceful and chaste
as a chamber of medieval sculpture.
Underneath the tedious quiet
their emotions, their psyches tangle
like limbs beneath sheets
fleshy and theatrical as porn.

Agoraphobia

Away from her dear home,
seven blocks from her house
the streets buckle
and facades of buildings diagonal themselves
inward, toward her,
creating a tunnel surrounding her
where underwater sounds
infiltrate and echo in her skull
and each step she takes
takes her into a staircase labyrinth
mazing her in a freewheeling prison
of spiked walkways,
of fumes lifting from sidewalk slate,
of embarrassing breathlessness
prompting trickling perspiration
and her mouth's wet taste
and a shifting fear funneling
inward, toward her,
blanking out what's above her
thus protecting her from the world
even as it causes terror of the world
with its monstrous people,
its biting sounds,
as black and gray annihilate all other colors
and in front of her becomes behind
and behind morphs into in front . . . .

Infanticide

In a trance she can do anything:
transcend stress,
plan atrocities,
execute homicides.
At such times she stays hypnotized
and cannot feel,
cannot reason,
cannot stop
the kooky melody in her head.
It's a song that dictates actions
she cannot fathom
in the light.
But in the shadowed territory
she paws her way across,
like a crazed wolf
hungry in an icy landscape,
she does understand
the embedded message in night time music,
the destruction whispered in a breeze.
It speaks to her more clearly
than a husband's static voice
or the clawing demands of a child.

Weak-willed, strong-willed,
during some disorienting evenings
she hears the wind's temptations,
the unthinkable acts it suggests,
doable as treading a high tightrope
when she's in a trance.

III

Edge of the Sea

Someone drowned.
I can't help remembering the day.
A beach party, the atmosphere
at first buoyant, bouncing with laughter.
Then abruptly a frown darkening the sand,
my mom's shaking hands,
the energetic sun turning lazy
in a lead, cross-hatched sky.

Minutes managed to continue, to stagger along,
becoming a headache in the eye
or a mouthful of liquid
too tart to swallow.
I crawled on a blanket, a toddler,
aware a weight had descended.
As the adults dropped to a beach sheet,
clustered, hugged,
I fingered the rash-like texture of a stray black shoe
and kept vigil over the water.

The Fall

He just happened to be there,
his timing Mozart-perfect,
the slate sidewalk
more sacred than a shine.

The baby came plunging
from a crane-high windowsill
down   down   irreversible
as water spiraling a drain.
She tumbled—sizable raindrop
ready to splash
or a chunk of hail
speeding toward oblivion.

His head tilted upward
at that exact beat
to see the infant dancer
do her waltz toward death.

Had he not caught a green light
moments earlier . . . .
Had he not
casually stopped
to button his sweater at that spot . . . .
Had luck's directions
been a fraction less honed . . . .

But he was there—
Samson or Hercules—

stationed there by time,
and his arms stretched out
in a pope-like gesture
to break the fated fall
as the laws of nature
hold the hovering moon in the sky.

The moment glowed
for him and for the child.
That second created a shock,
then a grin,
and then became a promenade
featuring Destiny strutting,
wearing bells around its ankles.

In a Hospital Room

Like an alien life form, it stands
guarding the room from a corner.
Its face, a rectangular screen.
Its feet, pigeon-toed wheels.

It dominates space
trusting its moon-hued panels
and electric chair straps
to slice through air.

Impersonal as death
it doesn't mean to frighten.
Unyielding as a ceiling
it offers no comfort.

At least a ceiling
exists for a reason.
What is the purpose
of this stark contraption
heavy with hospital disquiet?

It breathes without moving,
like an air vent.
It thrives without growing.
How can it live
if fear doesn't feed it?

Storm

I.

When her mother died
the ground became quicksand.
She had been Ms. Casual,
Ms. Harmonious,
a sparrow flitting from limb
to limb while sing-chirping,
oblivious to accumulating clouds.

After the grim hands
sank her mother's casket down,
down into a sea of soil,
after the first thud of dirt
hit the coffin's ungiving cover,
she became a raven without wings,
a birch without branches,
a stretch of earth
exposed to lightning,
its piercing, unsparing bolts.

II.

A weeping willow tree
with its solemn tendrils
swaying oh so subtly
instructs her how to grieve.
Too heavy to respond
to the wind's heaves of air,
its purpose is to bear
the earth's gusts of sorrow

without giving in, breaking down,
without losing patches of bark-skin
or sad strands of frazzled leaves.

III.

Haunted by tragedy,
disabled by fifth act catastrophe,
she is now deaf and dumb
and strives to communicate
over chasms of silence.
Listen: in total quiet
something is always mourning.

Gales toss nests
then continue to rage.
Lashes of rain drum down, do damage.
She can't hear words of condolence.
She doesn't have access
to sign language or even hesitant gutturals
that can express
this numbness creeping from her toe
to foot, to leg, to thigh . . . .
No crutches will sustain her weight.
She hobbles, gravely and bravely.

Plath's Demise

On her own
at 6:30 in the morning.
No consuming distractions
such as infants, clinging toddlers.
No needy muse
barricading her attention.
No bogus hope
chaining her to life.

She has settled in a new country.
She feels comfortable in this territory
among stark gravestones,
amid stern crows offering strenuous notes.
She has planned to reside here,
rehearsed her residency
the way Poe formulated "The Raven"
long before he resurrected his pen
from the tomb of his pocket.

In her former land
she has left a pitcher of milk:
something to occupy her waking children.
In the nation she has traveled to—
this new kingdom—
her coronation begins.
The ceremony bestows incense and grace.
It feels fur-soft—a cloak,
a carpet to rest upon.
She never knew such comfort.

Sylvia, 1963

Fifty years dead
and you are still alive,
resurrection lady, Jesus bride
eastering your way over the Atlantic
to the U.S., to humongous Canada,
globetrotting to Rome,
to Tokyo, even—in effective translation.

When you placed the milk and cookies
near your sleeping children
then tiptoed to the oven-dominated kitchen
you knew you'd become
a cageless cannery
at liberty to fly past death—
as fumes rise, seep, escape
the confines of apartment walls.

When the medics found your body
you fooled them into thinking
you had departed down a chute
to hell or oblivion.
In reality, you were refueling
for a touchdown
on the soil of another century,
in the minds of those
yet to be born.

The Rosebush

The rosebush leaned against a fence,
a wood barrier, undistinguished.
An immense rosebush
lavish as an opera, with dark pink petals
exclaiming in the backyard air.

Its branches overlapped, entangled themselves.
You would not want to touch them
for the thorns.
You would smell their scent, then
pull up a chair and sit.

You would want to be that rosebush
even as it sprawled with its roots
disturbed by a storm,
halfway out of the soil.

The fragrance that bush gave to the world
would make it worth enduring
life as an exposed root,
baring all.

Demons

In that house with your collie and family,
prowling, banging around your furnace room
with their invisible fists:
entities, monstrously motivated.
Noising on tin surfaces, on steel,
hissing when in the mood
then lunging into a threatening quiet,
these non-human beings
want a child, a sacrifice, a soul.

They will resist your entreaties to leave,
your prayers to religious figures
to make these phantoms crawl away.
They have enthroned themselves in your home
as if it were the castle of Faust.
They will ignore
your tactic of ignoring them.
Their Medusa roots won't tear
when yanked; such fibers can't be snapped.
Your intruders shall never go anywhere
where you are not.
Get used to it.
Get used to them—
their bitter music,
their metallic sighs,
their unearthly screeches.

It's only a requiem.

Protection

The witch in the woods takes flight,
tangles with whirling branches
at the apex of birches
while she hoots out of her green mouth,
out of the side of her snout,
her face contorted.

Listen:
she calls louder than a gaggle of owls,
hawks, the ebony birds that thrive
wild in the Colorado scrub.
Even worms hear her,
shedding their deafness.
They burrow to escape
the possibility of witch-contact.

She ascends like a Madonna
but shall plop down
on hard ground, on gigantic stones,
the screech of her arrival
bold as Niagara.
Keep all doors closed
but know she knows
what chimney to claw through,
what couch you crouch behind
and where—at all times—you hide your children.

After the Diagnosis

Suddenly this spring
I am praying.
I am chanting to the saints,
the ones I believe in
and even the ones I know never really existed,
are mythological—
the Saint Patricks of the globe
enthroned in fantasy—
and also on my knees or on the brink of my seat
I am pleading to the ones that might be make-believe
and yet may actually have lived.

I cannot even remember
the names of all these beings;
they flash in and out of my head
as I scroll the internet's listings:
the saints of illness, saints of misfortune,
patron saints of patients.
They will protect me.
The process of praying to them
will see me through
next week's operation
and help me with
the traumatizing word "terminal" that terrorizes
like a tumor that won't stop growing,
will assist me as I strive to deal with
the throng of doctors, nurses, technicians
I am trying to respect
like an ant diligent across mud,

between weeds, over boulders,
struggling to love the terrain that sustains it,
the way a sick one
wants to embrace the onslaught of chemo,
squadrons of medics with their
stockpiles of chemo, chemo, more chemo
all at war with a malignant mass.

I am stubborn as cancer
as I pray for miracles of grace
to sprinkle from heaven,
crave divine intervention in the form of entities:
dead artists, saints, prophets, angels, deities
to soar to my aid.
Sweaty from concentration I have researched them
till they have become more immediate than
stings of piercing needles,
more real than cups of my urine
I have obediently delivered to the lab,
more graphic than vials of my blood
I have offered to physicians like a sacrifice.
I have reached the point of total belief,
humble but strong—Samson shoving columns.
Rays of divinity rain down.
I am cloaked in hope
like the patron saint of scholars
clothed in a nimbus.
Note my aura as it grows.
I have taken the veil, the path, the light
suddenly this spring.

Advice Before Surgery

You tell him how
at first it will seem
a game: blackjacks, say.
He'll ready himself,
not worried about the outcome.
Then you will explain
how he'll cry
five months after the operation
and will think he's weeping
for the family dog
hit by a car decades ago.
Further along, he'll believe
he's shedding tears over
the death of a relative
he barely knew.
Finally, drenched in the shadow,
the stain of an eclipse
he can't escape,
he'll realize the magnitude
of what he's been through
and his grief
will seem inadequate
and your map
will have no relevancy
for his journey.

The Procedure

A nurse, something in hand, leans toward you.
She peers downward
as she's about to inject its shiny tip,
sharply, into your penis opening.
Will it numb or hurt, or numb *and* hurt?
Suspense: a law of the universe
as commanding as gravity.

*

An IV supposedly sedates you,
yet your eyes widen with alertness:
you don't mind becoming
a jack-in-the-box of reactions, even spasms.
"Sit still," demands the voice of neutrality:
a technician at the right hand of God,
the Almighty, the doctor in tinted lenses
redolent of Gothic stained glass.

*

You have stripped from the waist down.
Unfazed by a flimsy hospital gown
and the Godzilla limbs of medical instruments,
you try a grin in these grim surroundings
and hum some Bach.
But you are not tranquilized by tunes,
fugues or catchy syncopations.
Your toes twitch in anxious rhythms.

*

Your feet look innocent, vulnerable
in socks missing shoes.
A wire taped to your thigh
and a wire hooked into your rectum
and a wire plugged into your penis
drape you like crisscrossing accessories
completing your attire.
When the bed tilts from horizontal
to vertical, you know the ball's begun.
The medical practitioners stand there as hosts.
You will pardon them for this masquerade
years from now (maybe).
Forgiveness: a law of the universe
as necessary as nitrogen.

*

The surprise of the doctor's swift move
as he inserts a camera
on a glinting needle
into your urethra,
like the shock of life outside the womb.
No wonder babies cry at birth.

*

You are not afraid,
you tell yourself.
You dismiss discomfort.
You are not in pain.
You are not,
you are not,
you are not seeing blood

as a gloved hand pulls and pulls
a wicked wand out and out of you.

*

You don't remember the screen image:
your bladder a movie
for the physician to review.
You don't remember the urine,
a lava, smoldering while in you, and
on fire flaming its way out of you.
Memory is useful
except when it is very useless.
Memory is an evil
your system has tried to purge—a vomit expelled.

*

Nonetheless, you recall some scenes
such as your mother offering you soup
in your favorite bowl,
the balm of that moment
more effective than the philosophy
(so quaint it's New Age)
that says, "Knowledge comes from suffering."
You have learned not to trust pain,
in any of its variations,
to give insights or endurance
or even a fabled purity.
Pain brings only one thing:
a spacious ethereal interval—
when it's over.

Scar Tissue

I.

I wasn't a jangle of nerves
until four days before the operation
when a well-meaning colleague
stationed in our workplace computer room
uprooted her rump as she
leaned over to my desk to say,
"You're not going to die."
My throat morphed
into a knot of fear.
The lump lingered, becoming a snare,
a raised zigzag.
Some wrinkles resist the iron, indefinitely.

II.

My doctor, safe and cushioned
in his office of K-Mart Monets,
liked to crack jokes.
But in a serious mode
a week before the surgery
he said, with a somber smile,
"You're doing better with this
than I would."
Not just a teeny weeny shift.
Rather, an avalanche rumbled.
Finally he let go of,
freed me and himself of
white-jacket arrogance.

III.

I imagined the procedure would compete with
the plunging vistas of the Grand Canyon
or the stare of Michelangelo's *Moses*
or the sight of pyramids italicized in sunset hues—
an experience immense, dizzying, dazzling.
Instead, I woke up.
The thing appeared to be over.
The world continued its rotations,
tracing circles in unconscious stupor.

IV.

Nurses proceeded with windup movements—
nurses and med techs and orderlies
and physicians and nurses' aides—
trained to their gadgets
like sparrows drawn to a feeder.
A certain number of pecks.
A particular way to poke.
A sway to the right.
A sashay to the left.
A sheet placed here.
A wire set there.
Just so.

V.

After my father was diagnosed
he stopped eating.
Cancer can seal the lips,
the whole jaw.
I, on the other hand,
gobbled everything in range of sight

and fingers and tongue.
Monstrous bites didn't satisfy me.
My stomach became a vortex,
my hands a tsunami.
Food can serve all kinds of purposes.

VI.

More of the aftermath:
Day followed undefined day.
They lacked diversity.
My mother asked,
"Getting your reading done?"
I lay and recovered,
calm as a bed of ivy
planted too low for the wind's impatience,
its toss and frisk.
Bombed-out city after a war,
I had only enough energy to feel
passively gracious,
to bow my broken awnings, my tumbling stoops
cordially, toward the specter of illness.

VII.

Even more aftermath . . . .
the rest of my days
will be an aftermath . . . .
I scan the world
and the remainder of my life
for evidence of joy.
The Psalms my mother urged me to read
cry, "Rejoice!"

I find it in the simple
unfolding of a week,
the ceremony of Tuesday followed by Wednesday

which results in good ole Thursday,
then slam bang it's Friday and then on to Saturday, and
finally Sunday: a rest and a resurrection.

After the Hospital Stay

He looked at me as if to inquire
whether I'd live for another tomorrow.
Was such an outcome possible?
He assessed me with irksome uncertainty,
his eyes exploding as they explored,
despite the operation's supposed success:
my independent walks along hospital corridors,
the victory flags I sprouted out of both my ears,
my surprising come-back to kitchen culture
when I cooked nutritious meals for myself
as I recuperated at Mother's house.

That gaze lacerated me
deeper than any surgeon's scalpel.
That stare didn't accept mere appearances
no matter how comforting. Yet . . . .
I should have known my nephew meant no harm.
I should not have felt a pang of offense
I'm sure showed in my face.
His expression as he browsed my mug
intermixed pure pity with inquisitiveness:
the question he didn't want to ask
and I wouldn't dare answer.

Counsel

In one of his sober essays,
Seneca wrote we should show restraint,
"we" being all of us:
you, me and even Seneca.

As my father lay dying,
I sat between him and a window
and peered at both of them:
the man draped in white blankets
as if that absence of color
were the color of death,
and the glass-framed scene with its flashy
crosshatching of branches over branches.

I appreciated Seneca's words
as they whispered in my head.
But I also felt grateful for the rooks
stationed right outside the window,
their non-stop chattering
amounting to a collective screech
issuing from elms, birches and weeping willows.

Gaze

It doesn't have to be a sharp poem.
It doesn't have to be harsh.
It doesn't have to be edgy.
It just has to tell the truth
about death—
your father's dying, for instance.

In your mind's eye,
look at him sprawled in his coffin,
dark and dapper, a regular Nat King Cole.
Don't avert your eyes.
Stop grinding your teeth;
nervousness isn't allowed.
Peer intently enough into the wood rectangle
to gather details to compose something
poignant, yet not sentimental, about his passing.
Remember his final December afternoon—
years, decades, eons ago—
too cool to be called temperate,
too pleasant to be considered cold.
Recall the toxic phone call you received announcing his
departure from this world.
Imagine his eyes: usually bloodshot in life
but clear in death, under dusky lids
shut like twin caskets
in the shadowed region at the rear of a church.
Note his expression: neither haughty nor meek.
That mug: butcher-shop grim
but holding on to its youthful appearance,

its workplace vitality,
with pit bull stubbornness.
Record how it makes you feel
to be older than he was
when he died,
to have battled beyond a tumor
he couldn't fight.
Muse about guilt, about survival,
about a widow, about semi-orphans.
Keep staring—
for a light year if necessary.
Then write about what you've come to know.

Nightmare Nights

      when I can't sleep,
my limbs twisting the knotted sheets
as wrinkled thoughts stay with me
through mad-slow minutes,
cancerous hours,
stay with me as I slip under
and over blankets,
try to heave heavy pillows
off my defeated limbs
as the tonnage of denseness
resists, resists,
strive to claw my way out of garbage dreams
and an ant's nest of problems
and an impacted toilet bowl of obstacles
and a mesh of preoccupations
I've knitted myself into,
yet mangled thoughts stay with me as I
crave a way to scrape a passageway out of
inoperable coils of myself
though I see the task as hopeless
causing me to think of Anna,
placing her head just so
in adagio slow motion
on the train track's icy altar,
and I allow myself to approve of
what she did.

The Subway Joker

When you slipped
and your leg plunged
into the dark indentation
between the train and the walkway,
you gazed upward and smirked
like a TV comedian
who'd delivered his best one-liner.

The subway car passengers
didn't find the incident so laughable.
Some of them cried out;
others looked in the opposite direction
not wanting to witness
the wicked seconds
they felt sure would follow.

Had the train started up
while your body remained
half on the platform,
half in the hole,
you would have been a disaster,
split in two maybe,
perhaps decapitated.

But you sprang out of that gap,
found comfort in a subway seat,
then nonchalantly glanced around,

ignoring how micro-close
you had inched toward
a nightmare as finale.

As if you'd won a game
by skillfully cheating,
your lips lengthened horizontally;
your vertical teeth glowed.
You lived, attempting the grin of ignorance,
signaling without meaning to
all you wish you didn't know.

After a Massacre

Hell isn't a place.
It is a mother's face
contorted by menacing throbbing
when learning of her child's murder.

No location is a holocaust
except the wrinkled nest
stretched across a mom's visage:
muscles flexing in search of a voice.

A countenance is a home,
a fertile dwelling, locating
the one address in the world
from which anguish can communicate.

About the Author

Austin Alexis was born in Brooklyn, New York and attended Adelphi University in Garden City, Long Island and Queens College (CUNY). He received his graduate degree from the Graduate Writing Program at New York University. He studied dance on scholarship at the Merce Cunningham Dance Studio and performed with a number of choreographers. He has worked in several capacities at the Lincoln Center Library for the Performing Arts, the Metropolitan Museum of Art, and The Museum of Natural History.

Mr. Alexis has taught academic and creative writing, as well as literature, at a number of colleges, including Long Island University (Brooklyn Campus), John Jay College (CUNY), and Hunter College, and currently teaches at New York City College of Technology (CUNY).

In addition to the Naomi Long Madgett Poetry Award, Austin has received a Bread Loaf Writers' Conference Scholarship, a Millay Colony of the Arts residency, a Virginia Colony for the Creative Arts scholarship, and residencies at the Helene Wurlitzer Foundation of New Mexico and the Vermont Studio Center. One of his one-act plays was selected for the Samuel French Short Plays Festival. His plays have been performed at Performance Space 122 and at The Vineyard Theater. He also won a prize in the Poets for Forest Competition.

His two chapbooks, both from Poets Wear Prada, are *Lovers and Drag Queens* (2007) and *For Lincoln & Other Poems* (2010). *For Lincoln* was a *Small Press Review* "Pick of the Month." His poems have appeared, both here and abroad, in such periodicals as *The Journal* (Ohio State University Press), and *The Writer*. Some of his film, dance and theater reviews have been published in *The Arts Cure* and translated into Japanese. In addition to his poetry and plays, he has published short fiction in a number of journals.

Austin Alexis is active in the New York poetry reading scene and has also read on cable television and on a number of radio stations.